Horn

101 MOST BEAUTIFUL SONGS

Available for
FLUTE, CLARINET, ALTO SAX, TENOR SAX, TRUMPET,
HORN, TROMBONE, VIOLIN, VIOLA, CELLO

ISBN 978-1-5400-4824-0

Visit Hal Leonard Online at
www.halleonard.com

World headquarters, contact:
Hal Leonard
7777 West Bluemound Road
Milwaukee, WI 53213
Email: info@halleonard.com

In Europe, contact:
Hal Leonard Europe Limited
1 Red Place
London, W1K 6PL
Email: info@halleonardeurope.com

In Australia, contact:
Hal Leonard Australia Pty. Ltd.
4 Lentara Court
Cheltenham, Victoria, 3192 Australia
Email: info@halleonard.com.au

CONTENTS

ALWAYS

HORN

Words and Music by
IRVING BERLIN

Moderate Waltz

ALWAYS ON MY MIND

Horn

Words and Music by WAYNE THOMPSON,
MARK JAMES and JOHNNY CHRISTOPHER

AND I LOVE HER

HORN

Words and Music by JOHN LENNON
and PAUL McCARTNEY

AND I LOVE YOU SO

Horn

Words and Music by
DON McLEAN

AND SO IT GOES

HORN

Words and Music by
BILLY JOEL

Slow Ballad, with much rubato

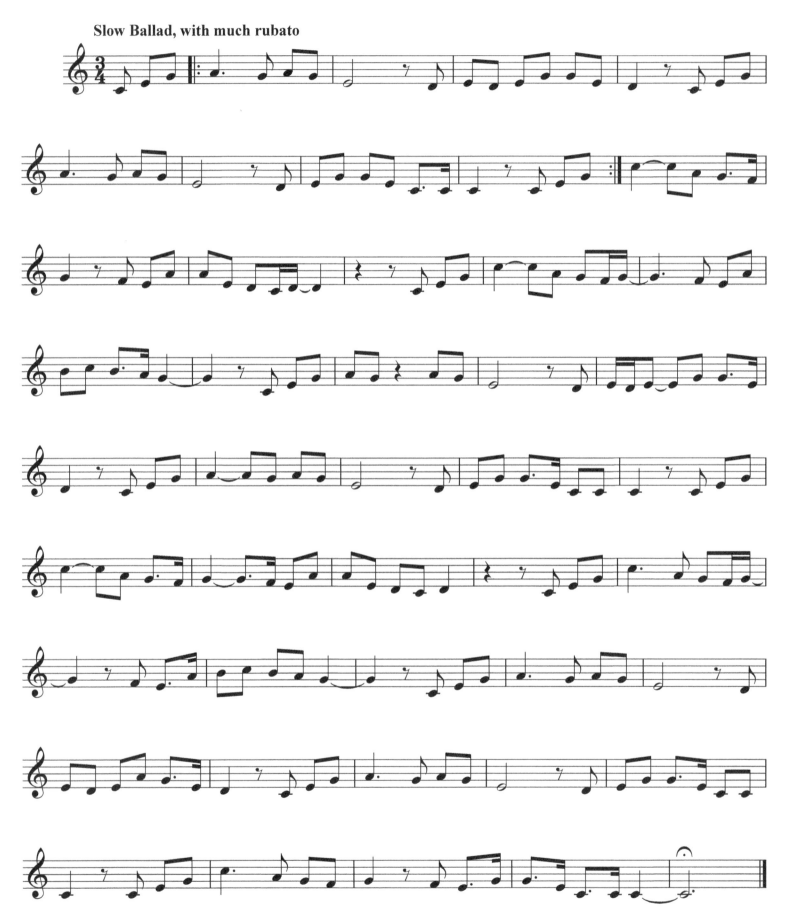

ANNIE'S SONG

HORN

Words and Music by
JOHN DENVER

Moderately

ANYWHERE IS

Horn

Words and Music by ENYA,
NICKY RYAN and ROMA RYAN

11

BEIN' GREEN

HORN

Words and Music by
JOE RAPOSO

BLACKBIRD

Horn

Words and Music by JOHN LENNON
and PAUL McCARTNEY

Slowly and smoothly

THE BOOK OF LOVE

HORN

Words and Music by
STEPHIN MERRITT

CODA

THE BOXER

Horn

Words and Music by
PAUL SIMON

BRING HIM HOME
from LES MISÉRABLES

Horn

Music by CLAUDE-MICHEL SCHÖNBERG
Lyrics by HERBERT KRETZMER and ALAIN BOUBLIL

BY THE TIME I GET TO PHOENIX

Horn

Words and Music by
JIMMY WEBB

CANDLE IN THE WIND

Horn

Words and Music by ELTON JOHN
and BERNIE TAUPIN

A CHILD IS BORN

HORN

By THAD JONES

(They Long to Be)
CLOSE TO YOU

Horn

Lyrics by HAL DAVID
Music by BURT BACHARACH

CITY OF STARS
from LA LA LAND

Horn

Music by JUSTIN HURWITZ
Lyrics by BENJ PASEK & JUSTIN PAUL

Slower

rit.

COME SUNDAY
from BLACK, BROWN & BEIGE

HORN

By DUKE ELLINGTON

CRAZY

Horn

Words and Music by
WILLIE NELSON

CRYING

HORN

Words and Music by ROY ORBISON
and JOE MELSON

Moderately slow, with feeling

DREAM A LITTLE DREAM OF ME

Horn

Words by GUS KAHN
Music by WILBUR SCHWANDT
and FABIAN ANDREE

DAUGHTERS

Horn

Words and Music by
JOHN MAYER

29

D.S. al Coda

CODA

EASY LIVING
Theme from the Paramount Picture EASY LIVING

Horn

Words and Music by LEO ROBIN
and RALPH RAINGER

ETERNAL FLAME

HORN

Words and Music by BILLY STEINBERG,
TOM KELLY and SUSANNA HOFFS

ETERNALLY

HORN

Words by GEOFFREY PARSONS
Music by CHARLES CHAPLIN

Slowly, with feeling

EVERY BREATH YOU TAKE

HORN

Music and Lyrics by
STING

(EVERYTHING I DO) I DO IT FOR YOU

from the Motion Picture ROBIN HOOD: PRINCE OF THIEVES

HORN

Written by MICHAEL KAMEN

FEELING GOOD

from THE ROAR OF THE GREASEPAINT – THE SMELL OF THE CROWD

Horn

Words and Music by LESLIE BRICUSSE
and ANTHONY NEWLEY

FOR ALL WE KNOW

Horn

Words by SAM M. LEWIS
Music by J. FRED COOTS

GABRIEL'S OBOE

from the Motion Picture THE MISSION

Horn

Words and Music by
ENNIO MORRICONE

GOOD NIGHT

HORN

Words and Music by JOHN LENNON
and PAUL McCARTNEY

GOODNIGHT, SWEETHEART, GOODNIGHT
(Goodnight, It's Time to Go)

HORN

Words and Music by JAMES HUDSON
and CALVIN CARTER

HAVE I TOLD YOU LATELY

HORN

Words and Music by
VAN MORRISON

HELLO

HORN

Words and Music by
LIONEL RICHIE

Slow Ballad

HEAL THE WORLD

Horn

Words and Music by
MICHAEL JACKSON

(small notes optional)

D.S. al Coda

CODA

HERE, THERE AND EVERYWHERE

HORN

Words and Music by JOHN LENNON
and PAUL McCARTNEY

HIGHLAND CATHEDRAL

HORN

By MICHAEL KORB
and ULRICH ROEVER

Stately March, in 2

I HAVE A DREAM
from MAMMA MIA!

Horn

Words and Music by BENNY ANDERSSON
and BJÖRN ULVAEUS

D.S. al Coda

CODA

I LEFT MY HEART IN SAN FRANCISCO

Horn

Words by DOUGLASS CROSS
Music by GEORGE CORY

I WILL

HORN

Words and Music by JOHN LENNON
and PAUL McCARTNEY

Moderately

I'LL BE AROUND

HORN

Words and Music by
ALEC WILDER

Slowly, with expression

I'LL BE SEEING YOU

from RIGHT THIS WAY

Horn

Written by IRVING KAHAL
and SAMMY FAIN

Moderately slow

I'VE DREAMED OF YOU

Horn

Words and Music by ANN HAMPTON CALLAWAY
and ROLF LOVLAND

Freely

IN MY ROOM

HORN

Words and Music by BRIAN WILSON
and GARY USHER

LA VIE EN ROSE
(Take Me to Your Heart Again)

HORN

Original French Lyrics by EDITH PIAF
Music by LUIGUY
English Lyrics by MACK DAVID

JUST GIVE ME A REASON

Horn

Words and Music by ALECIA MOORE,
JEFF BHASKER and NATE RUESS

CODA

LADY IN RED

HORN

Words and Music by
CHRIS DeBURGH

Moderately slow

LET IT BE ME
(Je t'appartiens)

HORN

English Words by MANN CURTIS
French Words by PIERRE DeLANOE
Music by GILBERT BECAUD

LOST IN YOUR EYES

HORN

Words and Music by
DEBORAH GIBSON

LOVE ME TENDER

HORN

Words and Music by ELVIS PRESLEY
and VERA MATSON

LOVING YOU

Horn

Words and Music by JERRY LEIBER
and MIKE STOLLER

Slowly, with a beat

LULLABYE
(Goodnight, My Angel)

HORN

Words and Music by
BILLY JOEL

Rubato, gently

MIA & SEBASTIAN'S THEME

from LA LA LAND

Horn

Music by
JUSTIN HURWITZ

MICHELLE

Horn

Words and Music by JOHN LENNON
and PAUL McCARTNEY

MONA LISA

from the Paramount Picture CAPTAIN CAREY, U.S.A.

Horn

Words and Music by JAY LIVINGSTON
and RAY EVANS

MY FOOLISH HEART

Horn

Words by NED WASHINGTON
Music by VICTOR YOUNG

MY FUNNY VALENTINE

from BABES IN ARMS

Horn

Words by LORENZ HART
Music by RICHARD RODGERS

MY VALENTINE

HORN

Words and Music by
PAUL McCARTNEY

MY WAY

HORN

English Words by PAUL ANKA
Original French Words by GILLES THIBAULT
Music by JACQUES REVAUX and CLAUDE FRANCOIS

NANCY WITH THE LAUGHING FACE

HORN

Words by PHIL SILVERS
Music by JAMES VAN HEUSEN

NATURE BOY

HORN

Words and Music by
EDEN AHBEZ

NEVER ENOUGH

from THE GREATEST SHOWMAN

Horn

Words and Music by BENJ PASEK
and JUSTIN PAUL

A NIGHTINGALE SANG IN BERKELEY SQUARE

HORN

Lyric by ERIC MASCHWITZ
Music by MANNING SHERWIN

PERFECT

HORN

Words and Music by
ED SHEERAN

PHOTOGRAPH

HORN

Words and Music by ED SHEERAN,
JOHNNY McDAID, MARTIN PETER HARRINGTON
and TOM LEONARD

THE PLACE WHERE LOST THINGS GO

from MARY POPPINS RETURNS

HORN

Music by MARC SHAIMAN
Lyrics by SCOTT WITTMAN and MARC SHAIMAN

RAINY DAYS AND MONDAYS

HORN

Lyrics by PAUL WILLIAMS
Music by ROGER NICHOLS

Moderately slow

RELEASE ME

HORN

Words and Music by ROBERT YOUNT,
EDDIE MILLER and DUB WILLIAMS

Moderately slow

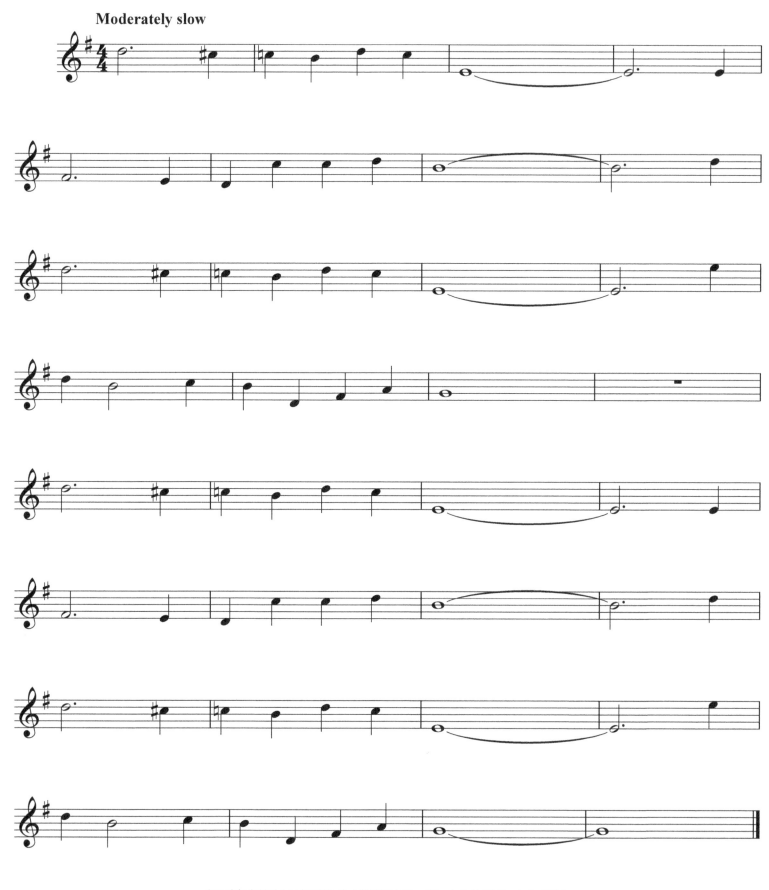

REWRITE THE STARS

from THE GREATEST SHOWMAN

HORN

Words and Music by BENJ PASEK
and JUSTIN PAUL

SAILING

HORN

Words and Music by
CHRISTOPHER CROSS

SCARBOROUGH FAIR/CANTICLE

HORN

Arrangement and Original Counter Melody by
PAUL SIMON and **ARTHUR GARFUNKEL**

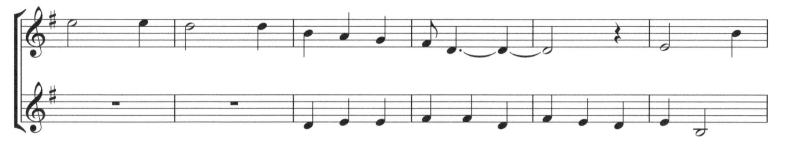

SHALLOW
from A STAR IS BORN

HORN

Words and Music by STEFANI GERMANOTTA,
MARK RONSON, ANDREW WYATT
and ANTHONY ROSSOMANDO

Moderately

SINCE I DON'T HAVE YOU

Horn

Words and Music by JAMES BEAUMONT,
JANET VOGEL, JOSEPH VERSCHAREN,
WALTER LESTER, LENNIE MARTIN,
JOSEPH ROCK and JOHN TAYLOR

Slowly, with a strong, rockin' beat

SHE'S ALWAYS A WOMAN

HORN

Words and Music by
BILLY JOEL

To Coda

D.S. al Coda

CODA

rit.

SMILE
Theme from MODERN TIMES

HORN

Words by JOHN TURNER and GEOFFREY PARSONS
Music by CHARLES CHAPLIN

Moderately, with great warmth

SMOKE GETS IN YOUR EYES

from ROBERTA

Horn

Words by OTTO HARBACH
Music by JEROME KERN

SOMETHING WONDERFUL
from THE KING AND I

HORN

Lyrics by OSCAR HAMMERSTEIN II
Music by RICHARD RODGERS

SOMEWHERE

from WEST SIDE STORY

Horn

Lyrics by STEPHEN SONDHEIM
Music by LEONARD BERNSTEIN

THE SOUND OF SILENCE

HORN

Words and Music by
PAUL SIMON

Moderately

STARDUST

Horn

Words by MITCHELL PARISH
Music by HOAGY CARMICHAEL

STRANGERS IN THE NIGHT
adapted from A MAN COULD GET KILLED

HORN

Words by CHARLES SINGLETON
and EDDIE SNYDER
Music by BERT KAEMPFERT

SWAY
(Quien será)

HORN

English Words by NORMAN GIMBEL
Spanish Words and Music by PABLO BELTRÁN RUIZ
and LUIS DEMETRIO TRACONIS MOLINA

TENNESSEE WALTZ

HORN

Words and Music by REDD STEWART
and PEE WEE KING

(THERE IS) NO GREATER LOVE

HORN

Words by MARTY SYMES
Music by ISHAM JONES

With emotion

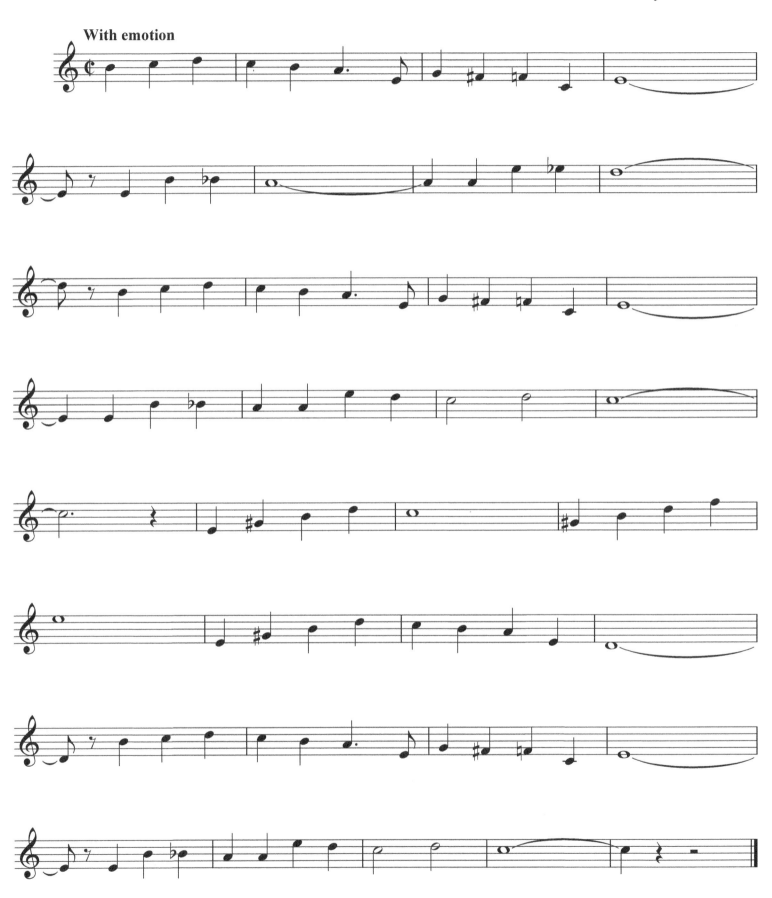

THEY SAY IT'S WONDERFUL

from the Stage Production ANNIE GET YOUR GUN

HORN

Words and Music by
IRVING BERLIN

THREE TIMES A LADY

HORN

Words and Music by
LIONEL RICHIE

TIME TO SAY GOODBYE

HORN

Words by LUCIO QUARANTOTTO
and FRANK PETERSON
Music by FRANCESCO SARTORI

(small notes optional)

TRUE COLORS

Horn

Words and Music by BILLY STEINBERG
and TOM KELLY

TRULY

HORN

Words and Music by
LIONEL RICHIE

UNEXPECTED SONG
from SONG & DANCE

HORN

Music by ANDREW LLOYD WEBBER
Lyrics by DON BLACK

(small notes optional)

WE'VE ONLY JUST BEGUN

HORN

Words and Music by ROGER NICHOLS
and PAUL WILLIAMS

WE'VE GOT TONIGHT

HORN

Words and Music by
BOB SEGER

WHAT A WONDERFUL WORLD

Horn

Words and Music by GEORGE DAVID WEISS
and BOB THIELE

WONDERFUL TONIGHT

HORN

Words and Music by
ERIC CLAPTON

YESTER-ME, YESTER-YOU, YESTERDAY

HORN

Words by RON MILLER
Music by BRYAN WELLS

Moderately

YESTERDAY ONCE MORE

Words and Music by JOHN BETTIS
and RICHARD CARPENTER

Horn

YESTERDAY, WHEN I WAS YOUNG
(Hier Encore)

HORN

English Lyric by HERBERT KRETZMER
Original French Text and Music by CHARLES AZNAVOUR

YOU ARE THE SUNSHINE OF MY LIFE

HORN

Words and Music by
STEVIE WONDER

YOU'RE THE INSPIRATION

HORN

Words and Music by PETER CETERA
and DAVID FOSTER

YOUNG AT HEART

from YOUNG AT HEART

Horn

Words by CAROLYN LEIGH
Music by JOHNNY RICHARDS

YOUR SONG

HORN

Words and Music by ELTON JOHN
and BERNIE TAUPIN